Copyright © 2016 Cassandra Washington
All Rights Reserved

About Cassandra Washington

Cassandra Washington is an experienced educator who lives and works in Chicago, Illinois. She knows the work and dedication of educators. She worked in the Chicago Public Schools System for 25 years. Cassandra's educational background includes B. A. in Political Science, M.A. in Teaching, and a C.A.S. in Educational Leadership.

Through her work as an elementary teacher, assistant principal, and principal, Cassandra knows firsthand the tremendous amount of stress that teachers and principals endure in their careers. Due to her experiences in trying to find a balance between work and home, she seeks to promote wellness and strategies to keep educators physically, emotionally and socially healthy. She believes that healthy teachers and students create spaces for academic success.

To help relieve stress, Cassandra enjoys traveling, motorcycle riding, photography, ballet and reading. She enjoys writing blogs: Chi-Town Principal and Sustah-Girl. Previously, Cassandra published an educational comic book, The Grammar Patrol. Also, she has led presentations at national educational conferences on social-emotional learning for school-aged children.

For more information, email her at:

cwashington@teachandtaketime4u.com

Table of Contents

WHY ARE THEY LEAVING?

THE EFFECTS OF STRESS
ARE YOU STRESSED?
Save Yourself!
Take Time to Relax
More Relaxation Techniques & Strategies
Heading Home
Take Care of Your Body
Make Important Decisions
RESOURCES

Teach and Take Time for You (TTT4U)

Introduction

  Teaching is a noble profession. Thousands of teachers go to work every day with the notion that they can save the world. They give it all, 110% every day, every year and for every child. As a teacher sometimes, one spends more time with their students than with their own families. Time at home is spent planning lessons, calling parents, completing reports, reviewing data and grading papers. Does this sound like someone you know personally? Is this familiar? Is this your life?

  You probably are having some flashbacks right now. You're thinking about all of the hours you spend being a teacher/educator or administrator, instead of being an average person with a healthy life. Are you feeling pangs of guilt because you know that your students need you? What would they do without you, their teacher? You love your students and care about every facet of their lives. But, people outside of the profession do not know the pressure and stress that goes with your dedication.

They do not know what it is like to be in a classroom with 30 little ones for six or seven hours. The public does not know what it is like to handle all of those little personalities and try to teach at the same time. They have no idea what it is like to be in a classroom with 25-30 thirteen-year-olds. They do not know that you often go to work sick because you do not want to miss a day away from your students. Or they do not know that you sometimes miss your own child's soccer game or dance recital because you are coaching or working with your students. There is so much more to the job that people don't have a clue about it. It would take hours to describe it all.

Well, I can relate to it all because I like you have lived it. I loved being an educator and started my career in 1991. In my life, I've had the opportunity to work in a couple of industries before education. Feels like I have been working many, many years. I was one of those high school kids who wanted her own money, so I worked part-time in a downtown office doing clerical work at Encyclopedia Brittanica, a publishing company. Throughout college, I did part-time jobs to keep money in my pocket and pay tuition. I graduated from college in the early 80's when jobs were hard to find, but I returned to that same publishing company and worked in customer service. Later I did bookkeeping for a restaurant company in Chicago. That didn't last long because my wanderlust was calling. Then, I jumped at the opportunity to live and work in foreign country. I worked in travel for Club Med as a G.O. (Gentil Organiser). Upon returning to the U.S., I worked in advertising for two big ad agencies in marketing research. My liberal arts education came in handy!

    I'm sure you wonder, when did this woman get into teaching. Please note that all of the previous experiences made me a better teacher and administrator. After working in the other world called corporate, and being laid off from an ad agency, I became a substitute teacher in the Chicago Public Schools. I had to pay the rent! Subbing is not an easy task, as some of you know; however,

I decided to get a teaching degree. I enter a graduate program to get a Master of Arts in Teaching at National-Louis University. In 18 months I received my degree and got my first teaching job. I was so excited for the opportunity!

I received a call from a principal of an elementary school that she was looking for someone to take over a classroom in the middle of the school year. The teacher was taking a leave of absence, and she needed someone quick and in a hurry. She needed someone who spoke Spanish. Well, I spoke some Spanish but not fluently. She asked me to say something in Spanish. I was able to talk and respond in Spanish to the principal's questions. She said, "you're hired." I asked, "What is the name of the school? Where are you located? What grade is this position? Do you want to see my portfolio?" The principal asked, "Do you want the job?"

Of course, I wanted the job. Well, the job was across town, at least an hour drive. It was a fourth grade bilingual/ESL class with approximately 35-40 ethnically, culturally diverse students. Talk about being thrown into the trenches! I didn't care because I wanted to teach.

This job was the beginning of my journey as a teacher. It was 1992, and I was thrown in the trenches. I was a soldier after boot camp, shipped to the battlefield without an orientation or a mentor to help me navigate what was going on. Of course, coming out of my graduate program, I knew everything including all of the best practices and theories. Well there's truth in the trenches and coming out of school, I didn't know much at all. Thankfully, some seasoned teachers were there to help out a first-year teacher. To this day, I am so thankful for their support and helping me through my first teaching job.

Mind you; this was the early 1990's so it was before everything was online. There were things like attendance books, written lesson plans, manually averaging grades and calling parents on the telephone. Fortunately, I had very supportive administrators and colleagues, and I remained at that school for five years. During that time, I also taught reading to seventh and eighth graders on the weekends. I was a worker bee. You name it; I worked it: after-school programs, tutoring, summer school, etc.

As an educator on fire, I pushed myself to return to school to complete another Certificate of Advanced Studies Program in educational leadership. The 18-month program prepared a teacher to become an assistant principal, principal or district administrator. Yes, I thought that I still knew it all and could easily be a principal. I was young, unstoppable and a change agent in the world of education. I did not have enough sense to know that it was also the beginning of STRESS in my life.

Upon completing the educational leadership program, I immediately began to apply for assistant principal positions. It was unbelievable, but I scored an administrative position at a highly regarded magnet school in Chicago. My colleagues couldn't believe how lucky I was to get an administrative position at such a prestigious, culturally diverse school. It is high performing in the Chicago Public

Schools system. I was so proud of myself for landing the job. What I didn't know was that this prestigious school was a bastion of politics, infighting, warring factions and more. For a moment, I was in my very own ivory tower because I was an assistant principal!

What did I step into? My naiveté was not prepared for what the next four years would bring. Again, I landed in the trenches after basic training. Learn on the job, put out fires, day-to-day operations, teacher meetings, parent meetings, teacher observations, after-school events, community events, budgets, 1600 students, 40 busses, remaining professional and long drives to and from work. EVERYDAY!

After four years, I left the prestigious magnet school for an excellent small magnet school, ten minutes from my house. What a wonderful place to work. I worked with a great principal, students, parents, and staff. I had experience under my belt, so this time I was ready for anything and everything! Yes, there were the day-to-day things to deal with, but I still carried stress around. To me, stress was unavoidable because as an educator it is and was all about the kids. What I didn't realize at the time was how stress slowly takes a toll on your mind, body, and soul. I stayed at my beautiful, small school for eight years until I was recruited to become a principal at another school.

From the time I became a teacher, my goal was to become a principal. Yes, I wanted to run my school, with my students and staff. I wanted to be the jefe (chief of the school). I am the master educator! Politics, funding and all that stuff that gets in the way would have no place in a building that I run. My nature is to dream big, nurture, and protect my students and staff. Well, that's the nature of all teachers, but it takes a toll.

As principal, I headed to my new school with a plan. It was a great plan, well thought out and on paper. Thrown in the trenches once again, I put on my armor. As principal, I could not defer any decisions to someone else. I had to always be on my toes. All the things I did as an assistant principal multiplied by three, plus some more. All kinds of things started to happen.

I gained weight, stopped exercising, ate the wrong things, worked 13-14 hour days, snapped on my significant other, couldn't sleep and much more. I did not have high blood pressure or high cholesterol before I became an educator! Plus, I didn't have gray hair when I first became a principal. Now, salt & pepper hair covers my head. Thank god for good skin and no wrinkles. Be careful what you ask for or be prepared for the weight of the education world was on my shoulders.

Have you felt that weight on your shoulders? Because you're a dedicated and hardworking educator, that pressure can be too much to carry around. The toll the job takes on you can be too much to bear. One day that toll almost took my life. The stress wreaked havoc on my health. One day, I was in hypertensive crisis and on the verge of having a stroke. I do not want this to happen to any teacher or principal.

There are ways to release some of that tension. I know that you're probably saying that I am one to talk. You're thinking, that I couldn't take care of myself, so how can I give advice. It has taken me some years to figure it out, but the experience is the best teacher.

In this book, I'm going to give you some tips on how to teach and take time for you. Whether you're in the classroom or are a school administrator, I want you to stay healthy and stay sane. I don't want you to lose your mind due to stress, go postal or burnout. Too many excellent educators burnout and leave the profession. When great educators leave the school systems, wisdom walks out the door. Calvin Coolidge said, "Knowledge comes, but wisdom lingers. It may not be difficult to store up in your mind a vast quantity of facts within a comparatively short time, but the ability to form judgments requires the severe discipline of hard work and the tempering heat of experience and maturity."

The school systems of this country need you and your wisdom to stay a bit longer. Children and parents need you to make a difference in their lives. Now it is time to take a personal journey to relieve some stress in your life. So, let your journey to calm begin right here and let's make these steps together.

Chapter 1

Why Are They Leaving?

Is your spark still there when you enter your classroom? Is your spark always there when you open your principal office? Are your creative juices flowing? Do you jump out of bed each morning with a smile as you prepare to go to your school building? Do you look forward to seeing the darling faces of your students? How do you feel about going to work each day?

Write down your answers to each question on a piece of paper. Are the majority of your responses positive or negative? Be honest!! If the reactions are mostly negative, then perhaps you're beginning to burn out, or you're feeling somewhat stressed. Let's be real, principal and teacher burnout are real! It is important not to sweep it under the rug. Call it what it is, BURNOUT!

Teachers and principals are burning out and running away from the profession. How many teachers or principals do you know who have left the profession in the last five years?

How many new teachers do you know that left the trade over the previous three years? I'm sure everyone knows of someone who left teaching and never looked back. The statistics are not decreasing! More and more educators cannot take the stress and demands of the job anymore. They cannot handle the numbers games! They just want to teach and enjoy all of the teachable moments.

A study was completed titled: Public School Teacher Attrition and Mobility in the First Five Years. It is a study on beginning teachers' longevity. Specific data and statistics are on the website for the National Center for Education Statistics. The study took place from 2007-2012. Here are some interesting findings.

Among all beginning teachers in 2007-2008, 10 percent did not teach in 2008-2009, 12 percent did not teach in 2009-2010, 15 percent did not teach in 2010-2011, and 17 percent did not teach in 2012.

- In each follow up year, the percentage of beginning teachers who started teaching was larger among those who were assigned a first-year mentor than among those not assigned a first-year mentor (92 percent and 84 percent, respectively in 2008-2009; 91 percent and 77 percent, respectively in 2009-2010; 88 percent and 73 percent, respectively in 2010-2011; and 86 percent and 71 percent respectively in 2011-2012.

One in four new teachers is burnt out. They feel overworked, over-stressed and in need of support. If our new teachers think this way, exactly how do seasoned teachers think? Experienced teachers feel both stressed and demoralized. Both can lead to educators leaving the profession. What is the difference between burnout and demoralization?

In the article, "How Bad Education Policies Demoralize Teachers" NEA Today,

February 7, 2012, it states that burnout examines how an individual's personality, physical and mental health and coping strategies help to manage stress. Burnout tends to be characterized as a natural byproduct of teaching in demanding schools and leaves the problem of burnout as an issue of teacher personality and naïveté. Burnout is portrayed as a failure of individual teachers to conserve their personal store of resources.

In this article, Doris Santoro, Assistant Professor of Education at Bowdoin College speaks regarding about research she conducted. She states that demoralization occurs when the job changes to such a degree that what teachers previously found "good" about their work is no longer available. Moral rewards are embedded in the work itself. She also says that moral rewards are what brings many of us to teach.

For us, moral rewards are about making our students' lives and need a top priority or using our talents to change their lives for the better. We dream of making a difference in the communities we serve. We want to keep living that dream, but policies, mandates, lack of funding or resources and compliance issues wake us out of that beautiful thought. The dream state is so much better than reality.

Did you know that teaching is the largest occupation in our great nation? Here is another reality. Roughly, a half million U.S. teachers move or leave the profession each year. In 2013 there were 13 million full-time teachers. It means approximately 15% of the workforce moves or leaves each year. The revolving door of the teaching force cost schools billions every year.

Here are more statistics about the revolving door. Nearly one in five or twenty percent of teachers at high poverty schools leave each year, a rate 50% higher than more affluent schools. Turnover rates among white, non-Hispanic were 15%, compared with 21.8% among blacks and 20.6% among Hispanics. Minority teachers are disproportionately employed in higher poverty schools. Lastly, 40-50% of teachers leave the job within their first five years of teaching.

Not only do teachers leave the profession, so do principals. A fourth of U.S principals quit their schools each year. Nearly 50% exit in their third year on the job. High poverty schools suffer the most in this significant exodus. Almost 27% of principals leave high poverty schools each year. In more affluent districts the turnover rate is approximately 20%. Charter schools have a 29% departure rate.

Why are people leaving?

Teachers want:

- Input and voice into crucial decisions in the building that affects their job.
- Mentors or coaches to provide additional support systems.
- Ongoing professional development to improve their instructional practice and strategies.

- Improved student behavior and discipline processes.

Factors that are driving the exodus of principals are:

- Workload
- Cost - personal, psychological, financial
- Lack of autonomy
- A bubble of isolation - principals, can't go to teachers or supervisors to discuss issues or challenges related to the job.
- Lack of support and professional development that principals receive once on the job.
- Sink or swim atmosphere

WHEW! That's a lot of data to review! It may seem dismal to some, but none of us have to become a statistic. There are ways for us to keep our sanity. Yes, you can teach and take time for you, too. In this book, we are going to find out some steps to take so that you do not burn out or become demoralized. Are you ready to go on a journey to calm? Let's go!

Chapter 2

The Effects of Stress

Think about your everyday life. You probably perform under pressure and are on ten all of the time. Whether at work or home dealing with complaints, deadlines, frustrations or other issues, you may not realize how stressed you are. You may not recognize the symptoms or causes of stress, but you can take some small steps to reduce the effects of stress on your physical and mental state.

What is stress? Stress is your body's way of responding to the demands of life or a threat. Let's call it the "Big S". As educators, the list of demands of the profession is long and continuously growing longer. You can probably think of at least 10 or 12 requirements right now. In fact, you are making a mental list as you read this. Are you getting stressed thinking about that list of demands? It is okay, just relax for a few minutes!

When you are in a demanding or threatening situation, your nervous system responds by releasing adrenaline and cortisol. When your body releases the stress hormones, your heart may beat faster, muscles tighten, breathing quickens, and the blood pressure may rise. Your body is reacting to the situation and trying to fight off whatever the threat is. These are instances of extreme stress. Let's talk a bit about our bodies' reaction to everyday stressors or chronic stress.

    Experts say that it is difficult for our body to distinguish between daily stressors and life-threatening events. Daily stressors may include an argument with a coworker or your boss. If you live in a big city or urban setting, the daily commute during rush hour may send you over the edge. Sitting down to pay bills may cause you stress. Teachers may feel overwhelmed by unruly students, the piles of papers to grade, planning the Spring Assembly, or a meeting with a parent. Principals may feel overwhelmed by district mandates, lack of funding, meeting with the superintendent, or an annual evaluation. Again, you can create a list of things that are daily, monthly or yearly stressors in the world of education.

When you experience these stressors all of the time, it can lead to serious health problems. Stress can affect every part and system of your body. The "Big S" affects the immune system, digestive and reproductive system. It can cause high blood pressure, heart attacks, strokes and other ailments. The "Big S" will make you age before your time and can cause emotional and physical health problems.

According to the Mayo Clinic, there are common signs and effects of stress. As educators, we like lists, so here are a few lists for you to review.

Common Effects of Stress On Your Body

- Headache
- Muscle tension of pain
- Chest Pain
- Fatigue

- Change in sex drive
- Stomach upset
- Sleep problems

Common Effects of Stress On Your Mood
- Anxiety
- Restlessness
- Lack of motivation or focus
- Feeling Overwhelmed
- Irritability or anger
- Sadness or depression

Common Effects of Stress On Your Behavior
- Overeating or undereating
- Angry Outburst
- Drug or alcohol abuse
- Tobacco use
- Social withdrawal
- Exercising less often

Some experts divide the symptoms of stress by cognitive, emotional, physical or behavioral symptoms.

Cognitive symptoms include:
- Memory problems
- Inability to concentrate
- Poor judgement
- Racing thoughts
- Constant worrying

Emotional symptoms include:
- Depression or general unhappiness
- Anxiety or agitation
- Moodiness, irritability or anger
- Feeling overwhelmed
- Loneliness and isolation

Physical symptoms include:
- Aches and pain
- Diarrhea or constipation
- Nausea, dizziness
- Chest pains, rapid heartbeat
- Frequent colds or flu

Behavioral Symptoms include:
- Eating more or less
- Sleeping too much or too little

- Withdrawing from others
- Procrastinating or neglecting responsibilities
- Using cigarettes, drugs or alcohol to relax
- Nervous habits, i.e., pacing, nail biting

You either think that you see yourself or a colleague somewhere among these lists of symptoms. It is essential to recognize your stressors, but look out for your colleagues, too. For sure you know of someone who is continuously ill with a cold, flu or they are coming down with something. How often have you said or heard, "I need a drink after the day I've had"? Do you or someone you know self-medicate to relax? How many of you have watched a person you work with, age before your eyes?

Have you looked in the mirror lately? You may have noticed a few more gray hairs on your head or a few more wrinkles on your face. What are your signs of overload? Sometimes you may enter your house, and you just want quiet. You want to be left alone! You are thinking to yourself, "DON'T TALK TO ME! DON'T LOOK AT ME! JUST LEAVE ME BE, PLEASE!" Been there, done that and got the T-shirt. Your spouse and kids look at you cross-eyed when you enter your own home. The weight of the world is on your shoulders, and you just want that burden lifted.

Educators have many stories to tell about their own experiences with stress. Teacher Johnson has a tough fourth-grade class throughout the year. Sometimes the students just cannot get along, and their personalities clash. As an experienced teacher, she knows all of the strategies around classroom management. She tries all of her bags of tricks to create a calm learning environment; however, the students had other ideas. Every day there is girl drama, boys horse playing, arguments on the playground that spill in the classroom, and other behaviors.

Teacher Johnson feels like nothing works with her students. Every day, she spends a lot of time putting out fires instead of teaching. Instructional time is wasted, and district spring assessments are right around the corner. How is she going to get her students academically and emotionally ready for testing?

Teacher Johnson begins to dread going to work each day. She does not want to tell her principal about her struggles because she does not want to be seen as incompetent. She does not want to commiserate with her peers because they have complaints too.

Soon, she begins to show signs of stress. She is tired all of the time and constantly worried about her job and end of the year evaluation. At home, she needs a glass of wine every evening to help her relax. Sometimes, two glasses of wine take the edge off. She just does not know what to do.

One morning the Teacher Johnson awakens with hives all over her body. She is itching from head to toe and inside and out. She takes an over the counter antihistamine and heads to work. On the drive through the morning rush hours, the incessant itching continues, and it drives her crazy. She cannot take the itching anymore and decides instead of going to work, she better head to the doctor's office.

    Teacher Johnson experiences symptoms of chronic stress. Sometimes, teachers and principals are so used to being overloaded that they do not take the signs of stress seriously. Be aware of what your mind and body try to tell you! Feeling stressed should not be a typical occurrence in our lives. You must be emotionally aware of your body so that you are calm down, soothe and take care of yourself.

    Think about a time when you were on stress overload. What were some of the signs that your body sent you? Figure out your tolerance level and how much stress is too much. Check out the website, www.stress.org to review 50 common signs and symptoms of stress. It is eye-opening. Additionally, on this website you can take a quiz to determine how much stress occupies your life.

Chapter 3

Are You Stressed?

Now that you have taken a quiz to determine your level of stress let's talk about things you can do to decompress a bit. It is crucial that you begin to take care of yourself and have some balance in your life. Does your life consist of 80% work time and 20% of balance? If so, that is not a good sign. Let's take a look at Principal Anderson's life to see if any bell ringers go off in your mind.

Principal Anderson is the leader of a K-8 school in an urban setting. He leaves his home each day at 6:30 in the morning. He says goodbye to his wife and kids and promises to get home at a decent hour. The drive from home to the school is approximately an hour on a good day. If there is a severe storm or special event in the city, the traffic is horrendous. While in the car, he thinks about his list of things to do when he arrives at the school building. He wants to hit the ground running.

When he arrives, Principal Anderson checks the list of teachers who are absent for the day. He sees that there are several teachers absent and not enough substitute teachers. Now he has to make sure all classes are covered and rearrange the schedule to make sure all teachers get their mandatory preparation periods. With so many teachers out of the building, there are not enough staff members to cover lunch and recess duty. That means that he and his assistant principal must cover lunch and recess duty.

Principal Anderson sits down at his desk and reads his emails. He notices that he has three class observations to complete by 10 am, a webinar at 11 am, lunch and recess duty from 12-1:30 pm and a mandatory district meeting at 2 pm until 4 pm. Principal Anderson promised to take his son to football practice at 5 pm. It is a tight schedule today, and there are always some unforeseen emergencies or fires to put out.

At 8 am the students enter the building. Principal Anderson greets the students as they enter the cafeteria for breakfast. Then he goes to the main office to complete the morning announcements. After the announcements, the secretary informs him that two parents are waiting to meet with him. He looks at his watch and proceeds to meet with the first parent. He knows that he does not have much time before his scheduled class observations. He hates to rush the parents, but his schedule is full.

The meetings with the parents run longer than expected. Principal Anderson is late for his first observation. He knows that once you are running late with one session, it spirals downhill from there. Principal Anderson will need to reschedule at least one observation because it is almost time for lunch and recess duty. Just as he about to enter a classroom to observe, the secretary calls him over the radio. The fire department is in the office and ready to conduct a mandatory fire drill. Principal Anderson thinks this day can't get any worse!

His day does not get any better! He feels pulled in too many directions. He sits at his desk for a moment and there lies a stack of papers to be signed, phone messages need to be returned, and he needs a moment to breathe. His head hurts. His stomach is growling, and there's no time to eat. Principal Anderson looks at his watch again. He must leave now to get to the district meeting. Maybe he can pick up a sandwich on the way, but he may not have time. He does not want the superintendent to see him walk into the meeting late.

The district meeting runs late, and Principal Anderson is late picking up his son for football practice. Plus, he still has not had anything to eat. He is running on fumes. While waiting for his son to finish football practice, Principal Anderson answers emails and returns phone calls. Football practice is over at 7:30 pm and he finally returns home by 8:15 pm. It was a very long day!

Do you think that Principal Anderson has balance in his life? He left his home at 6:30 am. His day was almost 14 hours. When he arrived home that evening, do you think he had any downtime? He probably had to spend some time conversing with his wife and children. Can you relate to Principal Anderson? He probably does not realize how much stress he is carrying each day.

    Like Principal Anderson, you too are carrying stress with you every day. It is not healthy, and it's detrimental to your physical and mental health. You can think of many stories like Teacher Johnson and Principal Anderson. These two stories are real people. They are dedicated educators who are heading towards the Big S and do not quite know how to handle it. Let's now think about some ways that you can save yourself from the damages of stress.

Chapter 4

Save Yourself!

No one was made to work all day, every day. Here are several things you can do to help you stay mentally and physically healthy.

DO NOT TAKE WORK HOME!
Repeat that statement three times and then click your heels. Educators are notorious for taking papers home to grade. How many of you have a big bag that you use to carry papers, teacher editions, and the kitchen sink? Yes, that bag that you drop at the front door and leave in that spot until the next morning.
There is a joke about teachers having eight arms because they are always carrying stuff. Many teachers have a car trunk full of school stuff, too. There is not enough room for the spare tire or the grocery bags of food because of teacher editions, ungraded papers, construction papers, sports team

uniforms, etc. Clean it out and do not put any of that STUFF back in your car trunk.

You ponder to yourself, "how can I lessen my load?". You think that no one knows your plight. No one knows what teachers have to go through and how much work they have to complete. In some ways you are correct. Many people do not know your plight or the amount of responsibility that you have as a teacher. However, it is not about them; it is about you right now. Block everyone else out for now, so that you can FOCUS ON YOU!

Whether you are teaching a self-contained classroom, departmental classes or a full high school schedule, the number of papers to grades seems unending. Depending on what types of projects or activities you have assigned to your students, that amount of papers may multiply times two or three. You take them home and try to grade them while sitting at the dining table, during dinner, while the TV is on and even in bed. Sometimes, you give up because you just cannot take it anymore! You have to develop and implement a plan to lessen your workload at home.

Use Your Time Wisely

All teachers get planning or preparation periods. Depending on your district or contract, you are entitled to three up to five preparation periods per week. Each preparation period is 30 minutes, and for some districts, it's 60 minutes. Think about how you spend your time during your preparation periods.

During this time, you may spend time collaborating with your peers or in grade level team meetings. Other times you may spend time communicating or meeting with parents. Depending on how your day is going, you may use their time to decompress for a few minutes. How you spend the time is up to you. The question is how can you better spend your planning periods.

If you take the time and spend one or two planning periods per week to grade papers, enter grades on the computer or write lesson plans, it means less work to take home. Go into your classroom or go into a quiet space and find a table. Take a seat, spread out the paperwork, take out your pen and get to grading papers. It is okay to tell your co-workers that you have a schedule to keep and you cannot talk right now. Explain to them that you are trying to do more at work so that you do not have to work as much at home. Convince your colleagues that they should do the same. Grading papers at work, what a concept!

Schedule Time to Enter Grades into The Computer

Technology is supposed to make our lives easier by saving time and trees. Yes, technology has improved our lives, but it has also put a lot more onto our plates. All school districts adopted grading software that calculates both numerical and letter grade averages. You do not have to do the math yourself. However, now you must enter the grades into the computer. After grading the large stack of papers, you have to sit at the computer and submit a grade for each student. It is one more thing on your list.

Since you are now taking one or two preparation periods a week to grade papers, you can also take a one period each week to enter the grades into the computer. Entering scores or letter grades will not take as much time as the actual grading. While grading the papers, put them in alphabetical order. The computer software will have the students' names listed in alphabetical order, so as you are entering, you are going down the list, typing and clicking away. Do not forget to hit the Save Button!

Use Extra Work Time at Work to Work

Both teachers and principals usually work late most days of the week. They stay up to two or more hours after the day has officially ended. Teachers clean classroom, check emails, call parents, grade papers, wind down with colleagues, etc. Principals check emails, return phone calls, complete mandatory reports, check the buildings and extracurricular activities, etc. School administrators are pulled in many directions during the school day. It is hard to decide what to do next on some days. Both principals and teachers must play a game of catch up during the hours after the regular school day.

Let's be clear; you should not spend two or three hours after school each day. You are encouraged to go home and have a life! Imagine if you schedule or plan out your time during the one or two hours after the regular day. Plan the days that you will stay longer to complete extra work. Create a schedule of activities to finish during that time. Use the time to grade, communicate to parents, schedule meetings, complete reports and more.

Here is a sample chart for teachers.

Day	Time	Activity
Monday	3:30-4:30 pm	Grading Papers
Wednesday	3:30-4:15	Call Parents
Thursday	3:30-5:00	Lesson Planning
Friday	3:30	Go Home!

Here is a sample chart for principals.

Monday	3:30-5:00	Read emails, make phone calls, schedule appointments
Tuesday	3:30-4:30	Meet with Instructional Leadership Team
Thursday	3:30-4:15	Complete compliance reports
Friday	3:30-4:30	Clean Desk and File

These are just samples. You know what your responsibilities are and can create a schedule based on your needs. You can change the schedule based on your priorities. The point of creating a plan is to develop routines that will assist in creating balance in your life.

Of course, creating a schedule is one thing, but sticking to it is another. You will see that sticking to a plan will make your life easier and create some balance.

Plan Lessons and Units During Off Season

Planning lessons take much thought and time. Usually, teachers are asked to submit lesson plans to the principal or assistant principal on a weekly basis. Teachers, guess what! Reviewing and reading lesson plans take much thought and time, too. You write your plans while at home on your own time. School administrators review the lesson plans at home on their own time.

It goes both ways and it is on your own time! One thing everyone is trying to avoid is more work on your own time, so think about this. What if you write your plans and create units during your summers, winter break or spring break?

Yes, it is your time off! But imagine taking a couple of hours each week during summer vacation to prepare lessons and units. It gives you more opportunities to thoroughly research topics, activities or project-based learning. You can co-plan with your team members and communicate with the principal about your plans. It gives you more time to think about how projects and student work is presented and graded. It also provides you a level of comfort because you have had time to write great plans. You were not rushed for time. You have time to share and collaborate with co-workers. You still have time to tweak the plans. Most of all you are less stressed.

Reminder! Do Not Take Work Home
According to a survey conducted by Huffington Post (http://www.huffingtonpost.com/2012/07/03americans-work-after-hours-extra-day-a-week_n_1644527.html), 80% of workers take their work home. Here are some more interesting points:
- 68% of people read emails before 8 am.
- 50% of people check emails while in bed.
- 40% of people are still doing work after 10 pm.
- 57% read work emails during family time.
- 38% read work emails at the dinner table.

Not only should you not take work home, but you also should not take work stress home with you either. After a long day at the school, do you sometimes find yourself taking out your stress on you mate, children or friends? Taking your discomfort out on those close to you is a detriment to the relationship. Here are a few tips on how to minimize the damage that works related stress has on your relationship.

Keep Your Work to Specific Times and Location

Simply, if at all possible, leave your work at the office or school. Make an effort to work from home only in exceptional circumstances and keep all work-related items at your desk in your home office. If you must work at home, do not bring the work or laptop to the dinner table, couch or bed. Designate specific hours each day for home life only! Eliminate and dismiss distractions and focus on family and your relationship.

Develop and Implement Mobile Device Habits

Turn off the cell phone and tablet. How can you spend time with your love ones or decompress when you are continually checking the cell phone for emails, text or social media posts? How many times a day or an hour do you check your phone? Do you check emails in the middle of the night? Calculate those minutes and see how much time you are donating to that compulsive behavior. Converse and spend time with your family and friends!

Develop a Support Network

Your loved ones are great listeners and nurturers; however, they do not always want to hear about what happened on your job. Placing your job-related stress on your significant other is unfair and destructive to your relationship. Ask your wife, husband or companion how does it make them feel to hear your rants and raves about work. You may be surprised at the response. Find friends or mentors in the same profession that can help you manage the stress. That does not mean that you should wear them down, too. However, having someone to lean on who understands the same profession can increase your ability to cope with the stress or the job.

Get a Hobby or End of the Day Routine

Develop a routine the signals to you that it is time to leave the job both physically and emotionally for the day. Get a hobby or develop a routine that signals it is time to decompress or get away from it all.

Create a Quiet Space for You

Sometimes you need a space in your house that signals to your mind that it is quiet time. Teachers and school administrators have families, responsibilities, and lives outside of the job. You can run a classroom or a school, but you still must go home to laundry, changing diapers, cooking dinner, chauffeuring your kids to sports, dance, etc. Sometimes a big house can seem very small when all of that is going on.

Everyone in the house needs a quiet space. Men have man caves. Women have a reading room. Kids have a game room. See where this is going. Create a quiet area to unwind in your home.

Work stress is detrimental to your home life. Learn to manage your stress, not dump it on your significant other or friends. Do not even let the stress ring the doorbell to your house. If you follow these steps, your family will be happier and so will you.

Chapter 5

Take Time to Relax

The definition of the word relax: become less tense, rest or take one's ease, unbend, unwind, decompress, slow down, loosen up or to become less taut. When you are stressed, you become tense. You are wound up or on 10! Your muscles are tight and knotted up. Too many things are coming at you at once! You feel like you cannot slow down. You want to relax, but you have a long to-do list. When is there time for you to relax when your day goes from sunrise to way past sunset? You are an educator on a mission!

There are ways to relax throughout the day. While you are at work or home, there are small steps you can take to create your private relaxation station. You can create your relaxation habits and routines. Also, learn your body and emotions so that you will recognize the triggers of your stress.

There are techniques that you can use throughout the workday to help you relax. Dr. Herbert Benson, professor, author, cardiologist and founder of Harvard's Mind/Body Medical Institute coined the term "Relaxation Response." He wrote a book titled, *The Relaxation Response*, where he describes the scientific benefits of regular practice of relaxation. The daily practice of Relaxation Response (RI) can be an effective treatment for chronic stress.

    Dr. Benson conducted important studies in the 1960's and 1970's that showed that meditation promotes better health, lower stress levels, well-being and reduced blood pressure. As a result of his study, he introduced a technique called Relaxation Response (RI). If you want to read more about Dr. Benson's pioneering work, more links to articles and videos are provided on the resources page.

    According to Dr. Benson, the best time to practice RI is first thing in the morning when you open your sleepy eyes. Practice RI for 10-20 minutes. Dr. Benson believes that practicing RI once or twice per day is enough to counteract the response to stress and bring about personal, inner peace and deep

relaxation. Below are the steps of RI, taken from Dr. Benson's book, The Relaxation Response.
1. Sit quietly in a comfortable position.
2. Close your eyes.
3. Deeply relax all your muscles, beginning at your feet and progressing up to your face. Keep them relaxed [Relax your tongue - and thoughts will cease.]
4. Breathe through your nose. Become aware of your breathing. As you breathe out, say the word "one" silently to yourself. For example, breathe in and then out, and say "one," in and out, and repeat "one." Breathe easily and naturally.
5. Continue for 10 to 20 minutes. You may open your eyes to check the time, but do not use an alarm. When you finish, sit quietly for several minutes, at first with your eyes closed and later with your eyes open. Do not stand up for a few minutes.

6. Do not worry about whether thoughts occur, try to ignore them by not dwelling on them and return to repeating "one."
7. With practice, the response should come with little effort. Practice the technique once or twice daily, but not within two hours after any meal, since the digestive processes seem to interfere with the elicitation of the Relaxation Response.

*Choose any soothing, mellifluous (pleasing to the ear) sounding word, preferably with no meaning or association, to avoid stimulation of unnecessary thoughts.

RI can be a daily routine. You wonder where will you find the time to do RI each day. When you awake each morning, take 10 minutes to practice. If you have a family, you may want to get up 20 or 30 minutes earlier than everyone else. Starting out with RI is a wonderful way to start your day. Practice it a few times and then develop your routine.

You can also practice RI at school. Teachers, you can set a time aside during your break, planning period or during your lunch break. Find a quiet spot in the school building, close the door and follow the steps of RI. Principals and assistant principals, go into your office, close the door, turn off the phone and lights. Do not forget to tell the secretary that you do not want to be disturbed for 10 to 20 minutes. Practice RI a few times and then develop your routine.

RI is a great process that can also be taught to the students. It can be a school-wide initiative to have a learning environment where teachers and students know how to relax and calm their anxieties or stress. It is a powerful initiative.

Chapter 6

More Relaxation Techniques & Strategies

While a work, sometimes stress is triggered quickly. Depending on the what or who triggers the stress, your reaction may be one of fight or flight. Your response may be to hold in your anger, anxiety or emotions internally. There are some simple steps you can take to relax and calm down.

Breathe Deeply

Focus on your breathing. Sit in a chair and sit up straight. Close your eyes. Put your hand on your belly. Slowly breathe in through your nose. Feel your breath start in your abdomen and work its way to the top of your head. Now reverse and exhale through your mouth. Try this for five to seven minutes. Breath deeply to slow down your heart rate and lower blood pressure.

Be Present

Don't be in a hurry. Slow down! Take a few minutes to focus on your behavior. Be aware of your surroundings. Be mindful of all of your senses. Notice the sounds and scents around you. Notice textures of things in your office or classroom. Notice the taste of the food you are eating. Take it all in and focus on your senses. You will feel less tense.

Socialize

Communicate! Do not live or work in a bubble. Talking face to face with a coworker or friend is a great way to relieve stress. Share and collaborate ideas or how to problem solve. Make connections with others who can relate to what you are experiencing.

Know Your Body

Learn how your body reacts to stressful situations. Do a mental scan of your body. Are your shoulders and neck tight? Does your lower back hurt? What part of your body is tight or lose? Sit down in a chair and place your feet on the floor. Do a mental scan from your toes to the top of your head. Breathe deeply and let the breath flow to the tight spots. Focus and pay attention to those places. Continue to breathe deeply for 1 to 2 minutes. Repeat if necessary.

Humor Is Good for the Soul

Sometimes you need a good laugh. Laughter lightens the mood or your load. Watch a funny movie. Listen to a funny comedian. Have a conversation with someone who makes you smile or laugh. Tell some jokes and make others laugh. If they do not laugh at your jokes, laugh at your jokes. You will feel better.

Pump Up the Volume

Music can work wonders for your stress level. Turn on your favorite songs or something soothing. Whether it is classical music, rock, R & B, or country music, turn up the volume and sing your heart out. Dance like you don't care. Slow down for a moment and focus on the different instruments, the voices of the singers or the beats. Get in tune with the music and feel yourself calm down. Enjoy yourself.

Move It!
    Exercise your body. It may be difficult at work, but where there is a will, there is a way. In a school building, you can walk up and down the flights of stairs several times. Some buildings have nice long hallways that are fantastic for walking. If the gym is free, go in and run around for a few minutes. Get a jump rope a count how many jumps you can do in two minutes. You can stretch in your office or at your desk. Stretch your arms over your head and your feet straight out. Wiggle your fingers and toes. Roll your shoulders back and forth. Do a few head rolls. Learn a few yoga moves. Get it moving!

Write It Down
    Write down your feelings. Personal journals are a great way and tool to capture your thoughts and emotions. Some people keep more than one journal. You may have one at home or another journal at work. They are perfect for writing about your experiences whether good, bad or other. As an educator,

journals are great for writing about your celebrations.

Teachers, you can write about a particular activity or new lesson that you tried. You can write about how a child or children reacted to learning something new. Principals can write about some of their interactions with students, parents or staff. There are plenty of experiences throughout the school year that will allow you to be reflective and jot down your emotions. Also, if you are not a pen to the paper type of person, there are plenty of free journal apps that you can download onto a mobile device.

You Can't Do It All

Sometimes, you have too much going on, and you feel pulled in too many directions. Your list of tasks is too long. Ten tasks for one day is too much. Decrease the number of requirements you want to complete in one day. Choose the three most important and impactful tasks or projects. Create a timeline or schedule for the day to track completion of that task. Tomorrow, choose another three tasks or projects to complete.

Be Prepared

Routines are key to decreasing stress. Always being prepared helps to reduce stress. For example, you chose three tasks to complete for tomorrow. Well, Monday evening you should prepare all of the resources needed to achieve Tuesday's tasks. Same thing goes for your home life. Prepare for your clothes, kids' lunches and necessities the night before, so that your morning is less hectic.

Make it an evening routine for everyone in the house. At school prepare all of the materials and resources to teach a lesson a day or two before the teaching it. Have everything laid out so that the distractions and loss instructional time is minimal.

Clean Up

Are you surrounded by clutter? Do you have a messy desk, yet you think you know where everything is? Well, you do not know where everything is and spend too much time looking for it when you need it. It is time to clean up and create a clutter-free space.

Clear your desk of excessive and unnecessary paper, books, and stuff! File away important papers. Do not move the papers from one stack to another. You can scan documents and store them electronically. Clear your desk of little knick knacks that take more space than memories. You only need a couple of family photos on the desk and a couple of pieces of art on the walls. Take a look in the desk drawers, too. Surely, there is something in them to throw or file away. When your work area becomes clutter free, you will create a more peaceful work environment.

Less Distractions

Throughout the day, you spend a lot of time checking phones, emails, social media and voicemails. Turn off the distractions because they break your focus and attention what is important.

Make fewer Commitments

Remember, you cannot do it all. Stop trying! Take an assessment of all of the things you have going on in your life. Write a list and choose four or five things that are the biggest priorities.

Less Meetings

Educators know that there is always some type of meeting to attend. Be honest; some meetings are a waste of time and way too long. You can opt out of a meeting. If the reason for the meeting can be addressed via email or a phone call, then do just that. Put a time limit on personal meetings. Fifteen minutes is long enough for the meeting to start and finish. Cutting down on attending meetings will free up time to do other things in a more relaxed state.

Stop Working Late

Your time is essential to your well-being. Working late five days a week is not suitable for your well-being. It is not good for your personal or professional life. Your official work day has a start and end time. Of course, there are times when you need to work late, but set boundaries. When an opportunity occurs, and you must work late, do not work past 6:30 or 7:00 in the evening.

After a certain point in the day, your brain or body is in shut down mode. Your work capacity will decrease, and the special project will not be your best work. Put it aside and start fresh tomorrow.

Check Everything at The End

Before you leave work for the day, give everything the once-over. Check messages, emails, social media, etc. Jot down anything pertinent to do for the next day. Pack your things, turn out the lights and close the door. Walk to the parking lot, get into your car and drive home.

Chapter 7

Heading Home

Teachers and principals, your work day is over, and your car is in drive. Another day, another dollar. What a day! It was nonstop. Now, you cannot wait to get home and in a hurry. There is just one problem. Rush hour traffic is a monster! You are going nowhere in a hurry. You can feel your shoulders tensing up. You try deep breathing and then some soothing music. Why aren't you moving? Was there an accident? You cannot see anything that would stop traffic. You check the traffic channel on the radio. The traffic reporter must not know what's going on along the roads. The reporter is not sitting in the same traffic!

Do not panic. You have some strategies to use to reduce the stress. You are heading into your time now. Do not take work stress home with you because there will be more waiting for you at your house. Now let's talk about tips to reduce the stress that you can use during your personal time.

Take A Detour

You can do this on your way to the job or the drive to your home. Take a detour. Taking the same route day in and day out is boring. Every city or town has a scenic location within its limits. Turn left instead of right. Get off the highway at a different exit ramp and see where it leads you. You may discover a new hideaway space. Watch the sunrise over the lake or river. Watch the sunset behind the mountain. Drive to a local park or state park and take a walk. While in the park, get in touch with your senses and breathe deeply. By the time you finish the detour, you will feel much better and perhaps the rush hour is over.

Do Not Self-Medicate

After a long day or week, the thought of a glass of wine or cold beer sounds wonderful. You think about a glass of Merlot or Chardonnay and how you will sip it very slowly. Some of you think about the wonderful new microbrewery that is on the drive home. You stop to sip just one glass. It feels so good going down, that it melts the stress away. You have another and another. You are feeling pretty good now. Nothing like making yourself feel better, but self-medication is not healthy. You have plenty of positive and healthy ways to make yourself feel better.

Exercise
Something positive and healthy is regular exercise. The benefits of regular exercise or physical activity are:
- Exercise controls weight.
- Exercise combats health conditions and diseases.
- Exercise improves mood.
- Exercise boost energy.
- Exercise promotes better sleep.
- Exercise improves your sex life.
- Exercise can be fun.

When you look at the benefits of exercise, think about all of the effects of stress. Exercise combats stress. Physical activity is a great way to feel better, too. It is also a great way to spend time with friends and family or just to let some steam off. So get busy and take a dance class or swimming class. Join a basketball or soccer team. Find a running group or some friends to power walk. Get to moving!

Enjoy Your Family
    Educators spend a considerable amount of time taking care of children and families that are not their own. When you are in charge of a classroom or school building full of children every day, it is physically and emotionally exhausting. Often, you are too exhausted to give valuable time to your children and family members. Either you spend too much time at the job or bring work home leaving little time the most important people in your life. You missed school plays, soccer games, dance performances and wedding anniversaries because you made work a number one priority.
    Starting today, you will make time for family the number one priority. First and foremost, you are a mom or dad. Do not be missing in action from your children. One day

you do not want your child to ask, "Who are you?"

Set aside a time each day to spend personal time with your children and significant other. Have a conversation that is longer than five minutes. Find out what's new in their lives. What are their aspirations? What makes them happy, sad or angry? Read to or with your young children. Call your mother and father to see how they are feeling. Get the picture! Make your family Priority #1.

Hit The Spa

Going to the spa helps to relieve stress. Spas are not just for women. Men, you too can make a reservation for the royal treatment. Treat yourself to a 60 or 90-minute massage. Let the massage therapist rub the tension and pressure away. Guaranteed, you will more than likely fall asleep on the table. Get a facial while you are there or a sea salt bath. Scrub off the dead skin and start anew and fresh. Do not forget the manicure and pedicure along with a nice foot rub. Find a spa near you and reserve your spot. Do not worry about the cost. You are worth every penny.

Read A Book

When was the last time that you read a book for pleasure? Principals and teachers regularly read professional journals and books to improve instructional practices and strategies. Why not find a great romance, a mystery of Sci-Fi novel to read, too? Research the best seller in your favorite genre. Download the book on your tablet or order a paper copy. Curl up in a quiet space and crack the pages. Happy reading!

Get A Hobby

Find an activity that you enjoy doing, and it brings you happiness or relaxation. Some enjoy reading a good book. Others enjoy camping, cycling or crocheting. Fishing is a hobby that many say is very relaxing. Gardening and watching your seeds grow into plants and flowers is a joy. Traveling to different states and countries can be a great hobby, too. You can choose from many activities. Do the hobby that makes you happy. Remember, this is about you.

Create A Quiet Space

Scout your house or apartment for the perfect nook or quiet space. You need a sweet spot to call your own. It is a little spot where you can relax and revitalize your mind. Picking the right location for your quiet space is very important. It should be slightly secluded if possible and serene. You need a comfortable chair that is big enough to curl up or stretch back to relax. Find a side table to hold books, a glass of lemonade or a cup of tea. Do not forget a lamp or overhead lamp for nighttime reading. Lastly, you need something soft and fuzzy to throw on your comfortable chair. Refresh and renew your spirit in your quiet space.

Go On Vacation

Plan to take a trip somewhere in the state, country or world. Teachers have the precious time off that most professions do not. There is winter break, spring break, and summer break. Each one comes every year around the same time. It is a perfect time to get away, reflect and rejuvenate.

Three or four days away from the grind can do wonders for your psyche. It can be a road trip with a friend or significant other. Solo trips are fun too. Whatever fits your needs and your budget is most important.

Faith and Spirituality

Faith and spirituality are not subjects discussed in the education profession. They are genuinely personal and in the eye of the beholder. Whatever your religious background and belief are, when under tremendous stress you need something to fall back on. Finding your spiritual side can help you through some tough moments in your life. Having faith and spirituality can bring clarity and peace that you seek. Again, faith and spirituality are very personal topics in your life. Both are available to you to have and use in your life as you see fit.

Chapter 8

Take Care of Your Body

Our bodies are temples. Just like temples, our bodies must be maintained to remain standing. What are you doing to maintain your temple? Teachers and school administrators work long and hard hours throughout the year. Many do not take the time to make an appointment with the doctor, dentist or to get a vision exam. Appointments rescheduled again and again. Eventually, something in the temple starts to break down. After the breakdown begins and aches and pains are next. Again, appointments rescheduled again and again. One day, a visit to the emergency room will happen. Let's not let that happen to you.

See A Doctor

An annual physical exam should be the norm. Check the calendar and see when is the last time you have been to the doctor's office. Has it been over a year? Two years? Three years? When was the last time that you visited the dentist office for an X-ray and a cleaning? What about your vision? Can you see using the last pair of glasses or prescription? The lines are a little blurry, aren't they? Make the appointments now!

It is crucial that everyone is physically and mentally healthy. Making an appointment with the doctor is being proactive instead of reactive concerning your health. Most school districts provide great healthcare benefits to their employees. The insurers have hundreds of healthcare providers available to you. Each month you make financial contributions towards the benefits, so use the services. Plus, it is another way of taking better care of your health.

Check Your Vitals

While at the annual physical exam, get your vitals checked. Stress is harmful to your health and causes high blood pressure or high cholesterol. If left unchecked, both can cause other potentially dangerous illnesses. During you, doctor visit, expect him or her to check the following:

- History. The doctor will ask you about lifestyle behaviors, i.e., smoking, alcohol use, sexual health, diet and exercise, family medical history, etc.
- Vital Signs. The doctor will check your blood pressure, heart rate, respiration rate, and temperature.
- General Appearance. The doctor gathers information about you and your health by observing and speaking to you. He or she collects information about how are your memory and mental awareness. The doctor also looks at your skin to determine if it appears healthy. Also, he or she observes if you can easily stand and walk.
- Heart Exam. The doctor listens to your heart with a stethoscope to detect anything abnormal like an irregular heartbeat, heart murmur, or any other clues to possible heart disease.

- Lung Exam. With a stethoscope, the doctor listens for wheezes or crackles.
- Head and Neck Exam. The doctor looks at your throat and tonsils. He or she also looks at your teeth and gums. The doctor may exam your lymph nodes, thyroid, and carotid arteries.
- Other exams may include:
  _ Abdominal Exam
  _ Neurological Exam
  _ Dermatological Exam
  _ Extremities Exam
  _ Laboratory Tests
  　_ Complete blood count
  　_ Chemistry panel
  　_ Urinalysis (UA)
  　_ Lipid panel (cholesterol)

Other exams are gender and age specific. During the physical exam, it is the perfect time to discuss any issues, ailments, aches or pains with the doctor. Be very specific in your descriptions of what is going on with your body. Tell it all: who, what, when, where and how. It is not the time to be shy or secretive. The doctor can only assist or support you based on the information that you give.

Eat Right and Sleep Well
     Teachers and principals always seem to eat in a hurry. A teacher's lunch period maybe only 20 minutes. Some teachers must eat lunch with their students. Principals sometimes do not eat lunch because of their hectic schedules and putting out fires. To sit down, eat and enjoy a meal is a luxury for most educators. It is usually grab and go. Also, many educators do not heat a healthy breakfast either. If you are one of these educators, for most of the day your body is not getting proper nourishment. Schedule a time to eat each morning and afternoon.
     Eat healthy food to nourish your body and mind. That means eat the proper amount of vegetables, fruits, grains, proteins, etc. Yes, potato chips, popcorn, hamburgers, and candy are delicious, but should not be the

norm. Neither coffee, soft drinks nor energy drinks should be the beverage of choice all of the time. The body needs water, so drink it. All the things told to kids about eating healthy, say them to yourself.

Start planning your meals for the week and make a shopping list. Go to the grocery store with your list and stay out of the aisle where the unhealthy foods lurk. Only purchase what is on the list. Go home and start preparing healthy meals. If you are consistent in eating healthy food, you will begin to feel better and healthier.

Feeling better and healthier includes getting a good night sleep. Adults need six to eight hours of sleep each night. Educators are notorious for grading papers or completing reports until very late at night. Many of you awake early in the morning, work 10 or 12 hours and then arrive home to do more work. Your body and brain are on overload. Then when you get into bed, you cannot sleep because you are thinking about the list of things to do tomorrow. Or if you fall asleep,

you experience a restless sleep by tossing and turning throughout the night.
 Set a time and develop a routine to go to bed. If that time is 10 pm, then each night make sure you are under the covers. Turn off all distractions including cell phones, tablets, lights, radio, and TV. Put away all books, magazines, and newspapers. Do not even put them on the nightstand. Go to bed, close your eyes and breathe deeply. Sweet dreams.

Chapter 9

Make Important Decisions

At the beginning of this book, statistics were presented about teachers and principals leaving the education field. People have their reasons for exiting, but much is due to stress and burnout. It is not an easy decision to make, especially when one invest time and money in becoming a teacher or administrator. One must weigh the effects of stress on one's mental and physical health.

Your job and livelihood are vital to you. Whether you are beginning your career or have many years of experience, you invested much time, dedication and money. You are in it for the long haul. Educating children and making their lives better is a long-term goal. You must save them from all that is wrong with the world.

With this goal, you educators put heavy burdens on your shoulder. At some point in your career, the yoke will be too much to bear. At that point, you must make choices that you may not want to make. At the beginning of this book, you reviewed statistics about teachers and principals leaving the profession. As you read, in your heart you thought that you would never have to make such a drastic decision. Somehow, you believe that making such a choice will label you as a failure. That is far from the truth.

After all, you have read about stress, the triggers and effects, you may have to make that drastic decision someday. If so, it means that you recognize how important it is to have a quality of life. You realized that your physical and mental health could sometimes be fragile and pushed too far. You recognize that family is a priority and spending time with them is priceless. All of these things are an implication of success, not a failure.

Remember, a stressed and burnt out teacher or principal is not suitable for students either. It is difficult for a person to be competent in the classroom or leadership when he or she is on the edge of a breakdown due to stress. The last thing you want is to have a meltdown in front of students or your peers. You must also think about your disposition or behavior when dealing with family and friends.

One day the question arises, "Should I stay or should I go?" When the question arises, you must do a self-assessment of your life. You must weigh the pros and cons of staying or going. Consult with your significant other. What are the financial consequences? What is your life plan after leaving? If you stay in the profession, what things will keep you there and happy? What are things driving you out of the trade? Write down the answers to these questions in one of your journals. Your decision must not be in haste.

Before making a decision think about these questions from an article, 7 Questions to Ask Yourself Before Quitting Your Job on the website, www.everygirl.com.

1. Why exactly do I want to quit?
2. Have I tried my best to remedy any issues?
3. What's next?
4. Can I afford it?
5. What do I like about this position?

6. What do I dislike about this position?
7. What are my long-term career goals?

Be very thorough when making such a dramatic change in your life. No job is perfect; however, no role should bring about illnesses, chronic stress, etc. You need balance in your life. Throughout this book, you read about tips and strategies to help you bring stability to your professional and personal life.

Use what you have learned to create a plan to bring peace, calmness and good health to your life. A journey begins with a plan. Your journey to calm begins today. Let's get started on your plan to a potentially stress-free life.

Creating Your Plan to De-Stress

There are two types of stress: positive stress and negative stress:

- Positive Stress is good stress that comes from situations that are enjoyable, i.e., winning a sports game, winning the lottery.
- Negative Stress is bad stress that is harmful to the physically or emotionally to the body, i.e., doing poorly on a test, receiving a bad evaluation.

List recent experiences where you were stressed. From the list, identify examples of good and bad stress.

Good Stress

_____

_____

Bad Stress

_____
_____
_____

From your list, identify stressors and their physical and emotional symptoms.

Stressors	Physical Symptoms	Emotional Symptoms

Review your chart of stressors. What areas of bad stress are most concerning to you?

_____
_____
_____

How will you cope with and prevent the stress that is most concerning to you? Review the strategies and tips presented in this book. Describe your coping skills with the bad stress in the chart below.

Nutrition	
Sleep	
Exercise	
Support	
Take Care of Self	
Time Management	
Relaxation	
Prioritizing	
Hobby	
Other	

Stress Relief Action Plan

Here is another worksheet to assist you in creating a Stress Relief Action Plan. Complete the questions below.

Target Areas of Stress:
1.   3.
2.   4.

Impact the stress has on you:

Physically	
Emotionally	
Mentally	
Behaviorally	

What is your goal? What is the outcome you would like to achieve?

Reasons for Change:
_____
_____

What are some potential challenges or deterrents to achieving your goal?

1. _____
   _____
   _____
   _____

2. _____
   _____
   _____
   _____

3. _____
   _____
   _____
   _____

How will you accomplish your goal or outcomes?

_____
_____
_____
_____
_____

When is your start date?

_____
_____
_____

Will you keep a journal of the process?

_____
_____

How will you monitor your progress or success?

_____
_____
_____

How will you reward yourself for sticking to your plan?

_____
_____
_____

Weekly Action Plan Checklist

List and describe the type of stress you would like to reduce for the week.

Physical (PH)	Emotional (EM)	Mental (ME)	Behavioral (BE)

Type of Stress	Actions	M	T	W	T	F	S	S

End of the Week Results

_____
_____
_____
_____
_____
_____
_____

Quotes About Stress

"To achieve great things, two things are needed: a plan and not quite enough time." Leonard Bernstein

"My body needs laughter as much as it needs tears. Both are cleansers of stress." Mahogany SilverRain

"Where'd the days go, when all we did was play? And the stress that we were under wasn't stress at all just a run and a jump into harmless fall." Paola Nutini

"If you really want to escape the things that harass you, what you're needing is not to be a different place but to be a different person." Seneca

"I promise you nothing is as chaotic as it seems. Nothing is worth diminishing your health. Nothing is worth poisoning yourself into stress, anxiety, and fear." Steve Maraboli

"If the problem can be solved why worry. If the problem cannot be solved worrying will do you no good." Santiveda

"From time to time, one must release the grime built up inside them to free their emotions like the ocean. Suzy Kassem

"Live a good life. More smiling, less worrying. More compassion, less judgment. More blessed, less stressed. More love, less hate." Roy T. Bennett

"A man of calm is like a shady tree. People will need shelter come to it." Toba Beta

"The more tranquil a man becomes, the greater is his success, his influence, his power for good. Calmness of mind is one of the beautiful jewels of wisdom." James Allen

Resources

Websites:
Every Girl
    www.everygirl.com
The Muse
    www.themuse.com
American Institute of Stress
    www.stress.org
WebMD
    www.webmd.com
National Center for Education Statistics
    https://nces.ed.gov
National Education Association
    www.nea.org
Help Guide
    www.helpguide.org
Huffington Post
    www.huffingtonpost.com
Mayo Clinic
    www.mayoclinic.org
Teach and Take Time for You
    http://www.teachandtaketime4u.com/

Articles and Studies

Public School Teacher Attrition and Mobility in the First Five Years: Results from the First Through Five Waves of 2007-08 Beginning Teacher Longitudinal Study, National Center for Education Statistics, 2015

Rosales, John. "How Bad Education Policies Demoralize Teachers." *NEA Today*. February 7, 2012.

Stress Symptoms, Signs, Causes and Coping Tips: Understanding the Harmful Effects of Stress and What You Can Do About It, *The Help Guide,* www.helpguide.org. September 10, 2016.

Benson, Herbert M.D., *Relaxation Response*, Harper Collins 2000. Print

Kelly, Tara. "80 Percent of Americans Spend an Extra Day a Week Working After Hours, New Survey Says." Huffington Post, July 3,

2012. www.huffingtonpost.com. September 1, 2016.

Boogaard, Kat "7 Questions to Ask Yourself Before Quitting Your Job."
The Every Girl, www.everygirl.com.
September 2016.

Your journey to calm begins now!

Copyright © Cassandra Washington 2016

www.ingramcontent.com/pod-product-compliance
Lightning Source LLC
Chambersburg PA
CBHW060402050426
42449CB00009B/1855